Let's Take a Trip
A Living Desert

by Guy J. Spencer

photography by Tim Fuller

Troll Associates

Metric Equivalents

1 inch	=	25.4 mm
1 foot	=	30.5 cm
1 gallon	=	3.8 l
1 ton	=	.91 metric ton
1 square mile	=	2.6 square km
1 °Fahrenheit	=	-32, $\frac{5}{9}$ × remainder to find °Celsius

Library of Congress Cataloging in Publication Data

Spencer, Guy.
  A living desert.

  (Let's take a trip)
    Summary: Describes the plants and animals of the
Sonoran Desert of the American Southwest.
    1. Desert biology—Juvenile literature.   2. Deserts—
Juvenile literature.   [1. Sonoran Desert.   2. Deserts—
Southwest, New.   3. Desert animals.   4. Desert plants]
I. Fuller, Tim, ill.   II. Title.
QH88.S66   1988   574.5'2652'0979   87-3488
ISBN 0-8167-1169-0 (lib. bdg.)
ISBN 0-8167-1170-4 (pbk.)

The author and publisher wish to thank Christopher Helms and the curators at the Arizona-Sonora Desert Museum
for their generous assistance and cooperation.

Morning comes to the Sonoran Desert in Arizona. It is hot and dry. Parts of the desert are sandy and still. But much of the Sonoran is bursting with life! The Sonoran is a "green, living desert."

How do animals like the *coyote* live in a place where there is so little water? How do plants such as the *cactus* stay alive in temperatures of over 100 degrees? Let's take a trip to the Sonoran Desert and find out.

The Sonoran is big—120,000 square miles! Its southernmost point is in Mexico. From there, it goes northward into Arizona and California. Although some sections of the desert are flat, much of it is hilly. There are also many mountains in the desert region.

The desert gets some of its water when snow melts on mountaintops. Rainfall supplies less than ten inches a year in the desert. It rains during both the winter and the summer.

In the winter, rain and melted snow flow down from mountains and hills into riverbeds and gulches. Water is the reason the Sonoran is a green, living desert. Plants can grow, and animals can drink from small pools of water.

During the summer, the *spadefoot toad* comes out of its underground home. The little creature has been asleep for ten months, getting moisture from the damp earth. When it feels the pounding of the raindrops, it digs itself out of its home. Then it finds a newly-made pond and mates with another spadefoot.

In the hot summer, the water dries up. Often a thunderstorm fills the dry riverbeds, or *arroyos,* but the rainwater soon evaporates. The desert earth is dry again. Plants and animals that live in the desert must conserve water and energy.

During the hottest times of day, the *mountain lion* sleeps to save energy. Then, at night when the air is cooler, the animal moves about.

The *saguaro* (sa-WAHR-oh) is a cactus that is able to store up to 200 gallons of water! Its accordion-like folds swell to twice their normal size as the plant draws up water through its roots. Once it is full, the saguaro can survive for two years without taking in more water.

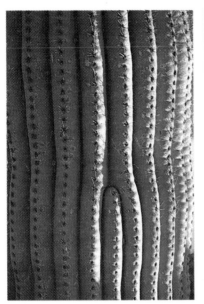

In summer, the noonday sun may bring temperatures up to 150 degrees! Tall saguaro and short bushes stand side by side in the heat. A saguaro may grow to be fifty feet tall, towering over a person.

What keeps the saguaro tall and straight?
Inside are woody "ribs" or "pipes." They are
light but very strong. The ribs help support
the weight of the plant, which may be as much
as six tons!

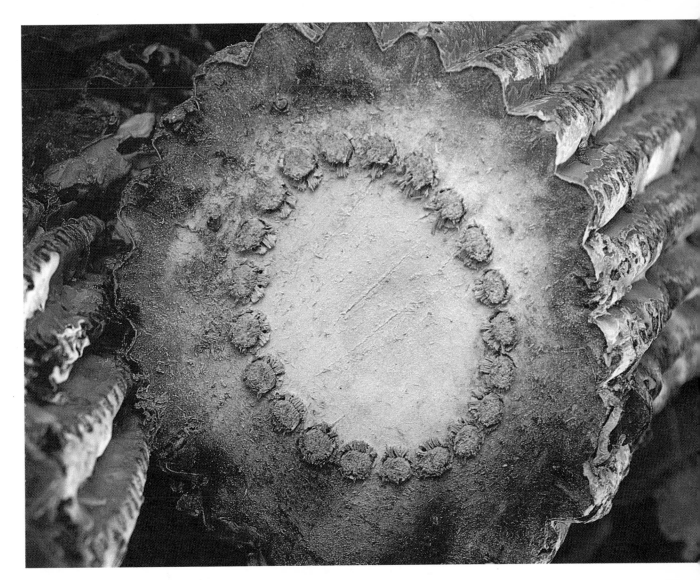

The saguaro starts as a tiny seed, no bigger than a flea. It takes about twenty-five years for the saguaro to grow to be one foot high. The saguaro produces its first blossom when it is just about fifty years old. The waxy white flower, once it blooms, lasts for only one day!

When bats fly out of their caves at night, they help pollinate desert flowers. Yellow pollen sticks to their bodies as they fly from flower to flower. The pollen then brushes onto the *pistil,* or seed-making part of each plant.

In the daytime, birds and insects pollinate more lovely desert flowers. You might even catch a glimpse of a butterfly—a beautiful desert sight.

Saguaro and other prickly plants are known as *succulents*. Their juicy pulps are a source of food and water for desert animals.

17

Spines protect the cactus from some animals by making the plant difficult to eat. But the *javelina* has a mouth tough as leather. It can chomp through a cactus, spines and all!

The desert has many kinds of plants and trees, such as the *Polo Verde*. Its leaves are small, so they need less water to survive in the hot, dry desert. Leaves are a source of moisture for birds, insects, and desert animals.

Birds are a common desert sight. They eat
insects, seeds, and fruit. *Gambel's quail* are able
to stand long dry spells on the desert.

The *golden eagle* gets its food from jack rabbits, cottontail rabbits, and other small mammals. As small creatures eat plants and insects, large creatures eat *them*. This process of survival has a special name. It is known as "the chain of life."

The *gray fox* climbs a tree to steal a bird's egg. A *white-tailed deer* looks for twigs. They have to watch out for the mountain lion, which stalks deer and smaller prey. The lion has sharp hearing and a keen sense of smell. It can spot animals in daylight or darkness.

A few *bighorn sheep* live in the desert mountains of Arizona. They can easily jump twenty-foot distances and scramble down rocky cliffs.

The pretty *Gila monster* is about one foot long and is slow and shy. If left alone, it will not bite. But when bothered—watch out. Its bite contains *venom,* or poison.

The *diamond-backed rattlesnake* is a common sight. It does not need to eat very often. The rattler kills an animal by injecting venom through its fangs.

The *tarantula* is a fascinating spider. It's the size of a small mouse. The tarantula isn't dangerous— it doesn't usually bite.

The *scorpion* is very small, but its poisonous sting
can be deadly! It prowls for insects late at night,
when temperatures are low. Desert insects such as
the scorpion can *camouflage* themselves. They
blend into the environment so successfully that
you don't even know they're there.

Watch out for the *teddy bear cholla* (cho-ya)! From far away this cactus looks like a cute, fuzzy teddy bear. But don't try to hug this teddy bear— its thousands of barbed spines can hurt you! The *organ pipe cactus* and the *agave* also have barbed spines. Keep away, but enjoy their strange shapes and beauty from afar!

The "tough guy" of the desert is the *kangaroo rat*. It gets moisture from seeds and never needs to take a drink. The *desert tortoise* gets its water from the moisture in grasses and desert wildflowers.

Would you like to catch glimpses of the desert close up? Let's visit the Arizona-Sonora Desert Museum! Many different kinds of cacti grow in the museum's desert garden.

And, the museum has two hundred animals, mostly in their natural settings. You may see two bears, rubbing noses. Or, a baby ocelot, crawling among rocks. And, if you're brave, you may have a chance to pet a desert snake!

The Sonoran Desert of Arizona seems peaceful at the end of the day. Wildlife that was sleeping is just waking up, as the sun sets behind a saguaro. Night-blooming flowers will soon open, and the desert will come to life. Listen closely! Perhaps you can hear the sounds of this living desert!